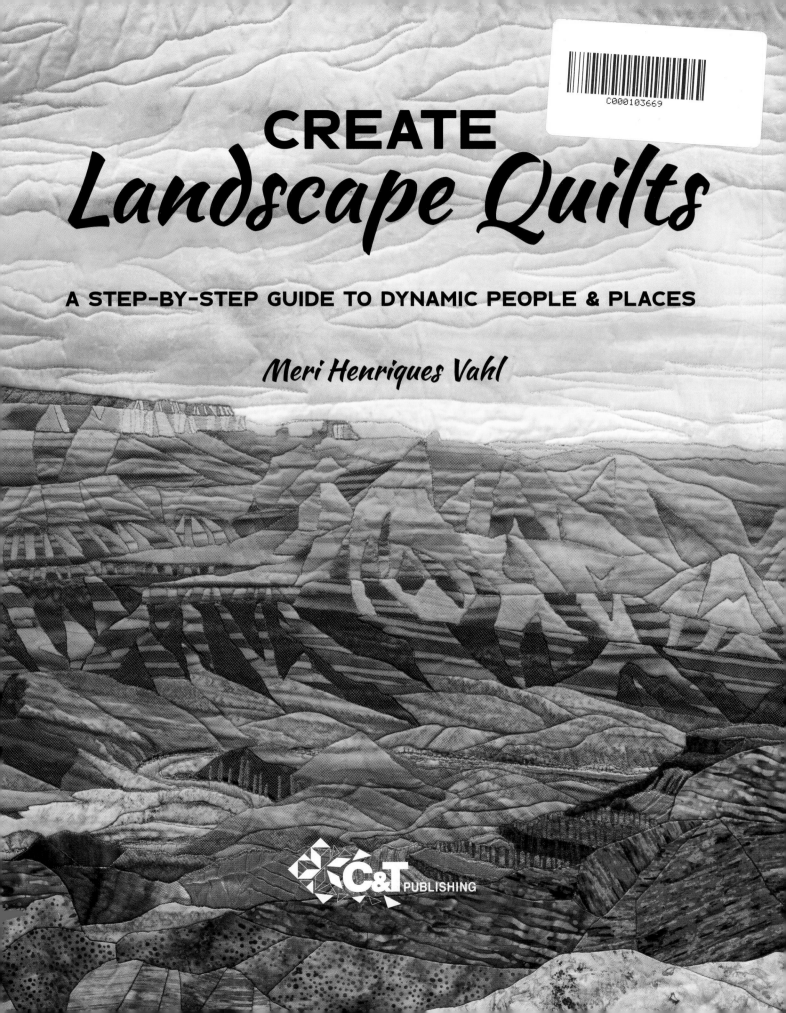

CREATE
Landscape Quilts

A STEP-BY-STEP GUIDE TO DYNAMIC PEOPLE & PLACES

Meri Henriques Vahl

C&T PUBLISHING

Publisher: Amy Barrett-Daffin

Creative Director: Gailen Runge

Acquisitions Editor: Roxane Cerda

Managing Editor: Liz Aneloski

Editor: Katie Van Amburg

Technical Editors: Linda Johnson and Gailen Runge

Cover/Book Designer: April Mostek

Production Coordinator: Tim Manibusan

Production Editor: Jennifer Warren

Photo Assistant: Lauren Herberg

Photography by Estefany Gonzalez of C&T Publishing, Inc., unless otherwise noted

Published by C&T Publishing, Inc., P.O. Box 1456, Lafayette, CA 94549

Library of Congress Cataloging-in-Publication Data

Names: Vahl, Meri Henriques, author.

Title: Create landscape quilts : a step-by-step guide to dynamic people & places / Meri Henriques Vahl.

Description: Lafayette, CA : C&T Publishing, 2021.

Identifiers: LCCN 2020027083 | ISBN 9781644030127 (trade paperback) | ISBN 9781644030134 (ebook)

Subjects: LCSH: Quilting--Technique. | Landscapes in art.

Classification: LCC TT835 .V34 2021 | DDC 746.46--dc23

LC record available at https://lccn.loc.gov/2020027083

Printed in the USA

10 9 8 7 6 5 4 3 2 1

DEDICATION To the memory of my dear friend, gifted artist, and ardent supporter, Ellen Edith, who always believed in my ability to succeed and who egged me on even when I had my doubts.

ACKNOWLEDGMENTS I wish to thank C&T Publishing for giving me the opportunity to publish this book, which my students have constantly demanded ever since I first started teaching. Sincere thanks also go to the kind and talented founder of Empty Spools Seminars, Diana McClun; Carolie Hensley at The Cotton Patch quilt shop in Lafayette, California; Gayle Wells and Suzanne Cox at Empty Spools Seminars at Asilomar, California; and to all of my wonderful and inspiring fellow art quilters and students!

Contents

INTRODUCTION

Traditional quilts weren't part of the culture I grew up in. In fact, the first time I ever saw a traditional quilt was in the early 1970s in a show at The Frick Collection in New York City. A friend had invited me to join her, and as we walked through the elegant rooms, we admired the many lovely quilts hung all over the walls and artfully draped over antique furniture and quilt racks. We had just stopped to examine a fine old quilt that was hanging on a wall when my friend grabbed my arm—really hard—and hissed directly in my ear, "Don't turn around, Meri! Don't look!"

Well, of course, as soon as she said that I *had* to turn around, and who should come walking into the room at that very moment but Jackie Kennedy Onassis! Dressed to the nines in one of her signature designer fashions, she was bracketed by two hulking bodyguards who just then resembled nothing so much as two Michelin Men because both were swaddled in dozens of quilts that Jackie had pirated right off the walls and furniture, although I doubt that was what visitors were supposed to be doing.

Noticing right away that she had an audience of two starstruck young women, Jackie looked over at us and giggled. "Isn't this fun?" she said—and then, "Oh, I'll have that one, too!" She pointed at yet another beautiful quilt, which one of her obliging assistants immediately scooped up off the chair where it had been displayed. With a final grin at us and another giggle, Jackie swept out of the room, accompanied by her hapless bodyguards, who were now even more burdened down than ever under heaps of her favorite quilts!

It wasn't until the 1990s that I discovered that there were other kinds of quilts besides the traditional ones. While visiting a friend and fellow Lamplighter singer in San Francisco, I noticed an art quilt hanging on her wall that was inspired by one of Gai Perry's impressionist designs. As a trained artist, I was struck by sudden inspiration: I, too, could paint with fabric! That revelation has taken me on a long and fascinating journey of learning and exploration to find out what other art quilters are doing all over the world, gaining a great deal of joy and inspiration along the way.

In this book, I would like to share my quilting adventures with you. I would especially like to share my favorite raw-edge fabric-collage technique with a fine tulle overlay, which I have had the good fortune to teach in guilds all across California and in France and Australia.

Quilt festival attendees and students alike have also been excited by the people I incorporate into my quilts, so I am going to show you how to make people for your quilts using the easy and foolproof technique I have invented for just that purpose. I realize that the thought of creating people can be intimidating, but I promise you that if you can trace a line, I can teach you how to make people!

The world of art quilting is an exciting and ever-expanding one, and working with the Fabric Collage with Tulle Overlay Technique and Paper Doll Technique is a wonderful way to join the movement. I hope you will enjoy exploring these exciting techniques with me as much as I enjoy sharing them with you!

Why Collage Art Quilts?

If you attend a quilt show and look closely at art quilts—no matter how different they may appear to be at first—you will quickly discover that many of them are done with a raw-edge collage technique. Many of these art quilts also incorporate fine tulle overlays, whether over their entire surface or only in certain areas. But why?

A tulle overlay on all or part of your quilt will give you the freedom to create anything you want without the struggle of figuring out how to make it happen. You can construct any image you desire while avoiding such fussy technical issues as drafting and piecing patterns, allowing extra fabric for ¼˝ seams, or figuring out how to create and fit your design together!

With a tulle overlay, you can incorporate anything that you can stitch over into your quilt: yarn, wool roving, lace, cheesecloth, cotton from your aspirin bottle, corduroy, velvet, feathers, paper, discarded thread, or even dryer lint!

Collage with a tulle overlay can be applied to any type of project (abstract, realistic, or geometric) and it is especially effective for landscape quilts. The fun part about it is that anything goes. There are no rules! You may decide to add several different layers of tulle to particular sections of your quilt as you progress through your creation.

I realize that this can be quite intimidating at first. If there are no rules, how do you even get started?

Several years ago, when I was teaching in France, I immediately noticed that my students were very uneasy and extremely cautious, hesitant to even pick up their scissors. Before long, people began coming up to me, photograph and several pieces of fabric in hand, to point at something in their picture, hold up their fabric, and ask, "What color is this supposed to be?"

"What color would you *like* it to be?" I would ask back. They stared at me in shock and confusion; however, after several similar exchanges, everyone slowly began to relax and get into the spirit of their work. I finally understood what was going on when my French assistant took me aside and told me that in her country, as soon as young children start going to school, teachers drum it into students' heads that there is only one "right" way to do anything, whether it's adding up numbers, constructing a sentence, or baking a cake!

Fortunately, our educational system has not burdened us with any such restrictions. If you want to make your sky green and your grass blue, or your grandmother purple with orange hair, and if you can pull it off successfully, there is nothing that says you can't do it! The tulle-over-collage technique will give you the freedom to let go of your inhibitions and play with your fabric to see what it—and your imagination—will encourage you to do.

I had my first exposure to this technique when I took a class with talented Northern California art quilter, Laura Fogg. I had brought a photograph to class, and once I had decided how and where to start working, I began constructing *Weeping Rock at Zion National Park, Utah*. I laid down my quilt back on my worktable and placed batting over it. To complete the first step, I ripped about a dozen 2″ fabric strips in a variety of dark browns and blues. I then overlapped the strips, allowing their shredding edges to soften the transitions and form the background.

Next, I placed five or six layers of brown, black, and navy blue tulle right on top of the fabric strips to darken that background and push it into the distance. I sprinkled on some random lengths of leftover thread ends and lots of fabric confetti to suggest the farthest-away foliage. Finally, I added the ledge and some fuzzy ribbon in the upper left-hand corner, which is where the "weeping" waterfall flows down.

Detail of tulle covering background strips in *Weeping Rock at Zion National Park, Utah* (See full quilt, next page.)

Weeping Rock at Zion National Park, Utah, 39˝ × 49˝, by Meri Henriques Vahl

For the foreground bushes, I was excited to discover that rather than having to cut out and design their trunks and branches, I could simply twist together two entirely different color yarns, gray and brown, to get the desired effect. I added fussy-cut leaves to disguise the blunt yarn ends.

A zillion pins later, I had secured a layer of black tulle over the entire picture, which I then hand stitched down using rainbow-colored Mylar thread to represent the dripping waterfall and lots of tiny crystal beads to suggest individual drops of water. A few more bright-green leaves were machine stitched right on top of the tulle that covered the foreground bushes, and the picture part of my quilt was done!

Because my quilt already looked so organic, I just couldn't bring myself to square up as Laura Fogg had recommended. (I will show you how to do this later in Finishing Your Quilt: Borders, Binding, and More!, page 96.) Instead, I constructed an entirely separate quilt out of two slightly different leafy-green batiks and attached the waterfall quilt right on top of it.

If you look carefully at the edges of the central landscape of the *Weeping Rock* quilt, you can see parts of the tulle layers overlapping onto the green batik under-quilt. You will also notice bits of raw-edge fabric peeking out all around the other three sides.

I encourage you to let your imagination run wild. If you can imagine it, you can make it happen. And when I say there are no rules, I really mean it!

Carefully observe what is happening in your photograph, and listen to what your fabric is telling you! Don't seek perfection. Allow yourself to play with your material. If you are open to giving it a try, the exciting techniques I am about to share with you will open up a whole new world of quilting for you!

Detail of tulle and raw fabric edges overlapping background quilt in *Weeping Rock at Zion National Park, Utah* (See full quilt, page 9.)

Where Do I Get My Inspiration?

People often ask me where I get the inspiration for my quilts. The answer is from anywhere that I can!

Although I have traveled to Guatemala twice and taken lots of pictures that inspired me to create two entirely different quilts, most of my ideas come from images in magazines and travel brochures, friends' photos and suggestions, and the internet. I am an enthusiastic internet tourist. The internet is where I can research images of places that I will never have the time or the means to travel to, and I can explore them to my heart's content. After my internet research, I think about all of the interesting things I've seen that have caught my attention. Eventually I fuse them into a single coherent vision that I can then turn into a quilt.

In 2006, and again in 2008, I had the wonderful experience of traveling to Guatemala—each time on a textile tour led by the brilliant Guatemalan quilter, Priscilla Bianchi. On both visits, I was dazzled by the people, the landscape, and all the brilliant colors. I told Priscilla that when I visited Guatemala, I felt like I was step-ping into a rainbow! And when I returned home, I knew I just had to try capturing that feeling.

On my first trip, I was fascinated by the women who live and weave in a tiny village called Santa Catarina Palopó at Lake Atitlán in the Guatemalan Highlands. Priscilla told us that the local people formerly wore white clothing decorated with small red designs and embroidery. Sometime in the mid-twentieth century, however, someone introduced them to a particularly lovely deep-blue dye. Inspired by the beautiful color, all the women suddenly discarded their white clothing and began weaving blue cloth for their garments! When our tour bus arrived in their village, we were greeted by a group of local women, all of them draped in yards of gorgeous blue fabric. They carried even more of it in their arms and balanced on top of their heads.

Detail of one Blue Lady in *Las Mujeres Azules de Guatemala (The Blue Ladies of Guatemala)* (See full quilt, page 82.)

Even before the tour ended, I knew that I would have to do something to commemorate and honor those women. I already had a vision of exactly how I wanted my quilt to look, but the problem was that I had no idea how to construct the ladies! After some serious experimentation, I arrived at the technique that I now teach and which you will find described in detail in The Paper Doll Technique (page 64).

When the central picture was complete, I used blocks of traditional Guatemalan woven fabric and embroidery to create the border. The end result was *Las Mujeres Azules de Guatemala (The Blue Ladies of Guatemala)* (page 82), which I feel celebrates not only the beauty of the women of Santa Catarina Palopó but also the beauty of their handicrafts. I have continued to make this a requirement when I create the borders for each of my subsequent internationally inspired quilts.

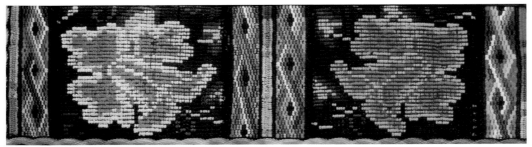

Border detail in *Las Mujeres Azules de Guatemala (The Blue Ladies of Guatemala)* (See full quilt, page 82.)

During my second trip to Guatemala, I was once again struck by the vitality and sights of the famous weekly marketplace in the mountain village of Chichicastenango. By now, I was solid in my people-making technique. But I had taken so many photos of the local folks who came from all over the area to sell and shop at the market that it was difficult to know where to begin and what to include in my new quilt. In the end, I selected parts of several different photographs to create the atmosphere of bright flowers, bustling activity, and people dressed in marvelous clothing. I was delighted and honored when *Flower Market at Chichicastenango, Guatemala* (page 64) won the grand prize at the Mancuso Brothers' Best Quilts of the World contest in 2009.

Detail of *Flower Market at Chichicastenango, Guatemala* (See full quilt, page 64.)

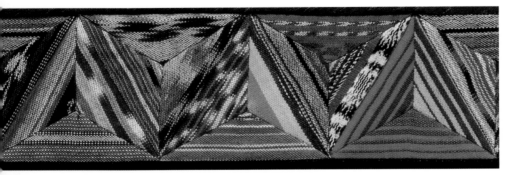

My quilts are not only actual fabric collages but also collages of the many images and ideas—the inspiration—that I have gathered from both my real and virtual travels, from magazines and travel brochures, and from friends' photos and suggestions. I always research any likely place, viewing as many pictures as possible to get a feel for the flavor of the setting: its people, their handicrafts, and the landscape. I end up selecting and piecing together elements from all the things I have seen and the impressions I have gained.

Let me make it clear: I'm not suggesting you should go around stealing other people's photographs off the internet or out of magazines without asking their permission. However, creating your own version of reality by selecting four, five, or more photos and forming them into a single unique landscape hasn't stolen anything from anyone as far as I am concerned.

Any quilt you make that is inspired by your research will never be an exact reproduction of the photographs you have viewed and worked with. By the very nature of the difference between photography and fabric, it can't be!

Let's take a look at the Fabric Collage with Tulle Overlay Technique that will allow you to realize your own travels, dreams, and visions.

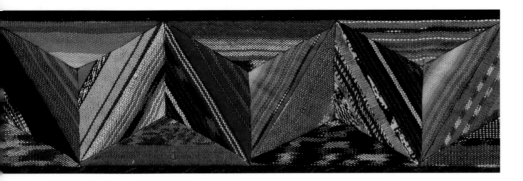

The Fabric Collage with Tulle Overlay Technique

This technique is extremely simple and is appropriate for all skill levels. You might even want to try it with a child!

Some experience with free-motion quilting, or at least having the willingness to experiment with it, is recommended. Since this technique is so flexible, however, it is possible to make a tulle-covered collage quilt using standard straight stitching only, which is what I did with most of my second attempt at landscape collage: *Beyond the Blue Mountains* (at right). Because I was just beginning to learn free-motion quilting, I began sewing with a bit of trepidation. I was unsure if I could really do it and if I wanted my stitches to quietly disappear into the background or enhance the visual image by adding new color elements to the picture. By the time I was ready to tackle the foreground, I felt braver, and I took my first experimental stab at machine quilting.

Beyond the Blue Mountains, 25½″ × 33″, by Meri Henriques Vahl

The inspiration for this quilt came from a photo in my yearly datebook calendar. Since I knew that it was going to be my *interpretation* of that photograph in fabric rather than a literal copy of it, I felt free to experiment. It was fun to play with the batiks, textured velvet, bits of fashion yarn, and especially the pleated green hill fabric. I was able to cut off and use the fuzzy selvage edges of that pleated fabric to form the tree lines on some of the ridges. Being able to improvise like this is one of the many joys of using the Fabric Collage with a Tulle Overlay Technique!

Detail of selvage used as distant tree lines in *Beyond the Blue Mountains* (See full quilt, page 15.)

Fabric Collage with Tulle Overlay is an all-in-one technique. In other words, you don't make a separate quilt top and then add batting and a quilt back afterwards. Instead, you construct the entire central landscape portion of your quilt—front, batting, and back—all at once, *except for the borders*. The advantage of this is twofold: Your quilt can be assembled more quickly than if you were using traditional methods, and by the time you are ready to begin stitching, you will actually be trapping the fabric beneath the tulle *and* quilting your project, minus the borders, all in one go!

I give a detailed description of the process on the following pages. I hope you will take a chance and experiment with this technique on your own project. If you would like even more guidance, I provide it in A Simple Landscape Collage (page 44), which takes you step-by-step through a landscape project inspired by a photograph I took of the Grand Tetons in Wyoming.

SELECTING YOUR PHOTOGRAPH

To begin, select a landscape photograph that really attracts you. If your photo doesn't speak to you, you won't enjoy making your quilt and probably won't even complete it. Students often bring several photographs to class and ask me which one they should choose. I always tell them the same thing: Go with the one you like the best. It is important to choose an image you love rather than what you think will turn out to be the easiest one to work with.

Don't worry about how elaborate or detailed your photo is. If you like it, go for it! Remember your art quilt will be your *impression* of that place. It's not a perfectly rendered reproduction of the photograph but instead a representation of how you *feel* about it. As you make your quilt, you can add as much or as little detail as you wish.

There is no need to enlarge your photo. It's there for inspiration so you don't have to invent a landscape design all on your own. However, some students are more comfortable drawing a full-size sketch of their landscape and creating freezer-paper pattern pieces from their drawing before they start constructing their quilt.

Remember: There are no rules!

 Tip If you do decide to make pattern pieces, you don't have to include a ¼˝ seam allowance all around. Just be sure to leave enough extra fabric around the bottom edges and, if necessary, the side edges so the next layer of fabric can overlap it on the quilt!

CHOOSING YOUR QUILT BACKING

Choose a piece of fabric for your quilt backing, making sure that it is a bit larger than what you want the finished landscape part of your quilt to be.

NOTE: *You don't need to include enough quilt backing for your borders, because once you have finished quilting, you will square up the landscape portion of your quilt. I'll show you how to add borders or even more quilt (see Finishing Your Quilt: Borders, Binding, and More!, page 96).*

Be sure to iron your quilt backing *really well* to get all the wrinkles out! Ironing the backing is very important. You won't be able to go back and correct this once you have started working on your landscape, and it is very difficult to get the wrinkles out of your quilt once you have started layering it together.

Place your quilt backing *facedown* on your worktable.

ADDING THE BATTING

Select a piece of batting that is more or less the same size as the quilt backing, making sure that any wrinkles are ironed out. Place it on top of the quilt backing. You are now ready to begin your landscape!

STARTING WITH THE ELEMENTS FARTHEST AWAY

As you go through this process, it is important to understand that you will be working—and thinking—in overlapping layers. There are no restrictions about how many layers there can be. All you need is to be able to stitch through them all when it comes time to quilt your project.

Take a look at your photograph and analyze what the different layers might be. Start working on whatever is farthest away in your landscape. It's usually the sky, but it could also be the green forest background behind the foliage and tree details that you will eventually add on top of the distant forest.

 Tip *Reminder:* Whenever you are making a fabric landscape collage with a tulle overlay, be sure to *think and work in overlapping layers!*

Whether you are starting with the sky, a forest, or a group of buildings, you will want to audition several different fabric choices for that background. You might also want to take a look at the fabric or fabrics you intend to layer on top of or around it to see if they are all compatible with each other. You don't need to pin or fuse anything down, which gives you the freedom to change your mind about any particular fabric once you see how it fits in with your other fabrics.

As discussed previously, it is important to iron the wrinkles out of each piece of fabric that you incorporate into your landscape. It is nearly impossible to get rid of wrinkles once a fabric piece is placed on your quilt!

Since there will be many more layers of fabric on top of the first background layer, the background doesn't need to cover the entire batting. Just place it on the part of the landscape where you want it to show. Add a little extra along the bottom edge so that the next layer of fabric will overlap it.

Continue adding landscape layers, always keeping an eye on how your fabrics are working together. You can audition fabrics before you begin or experiment and see how the different colors and textures work together as you progress. You can always change your mind and replace your first choice if you feel that another fabric or color would work better.

Remember to overlap new pieces over previous ones. You don't want the batting to show if a piece happens to move while you're stitching. If shifting occurs, I do know from personal experience that you can always use a permanent marker to fill in any offending gaps!

It's great fun to get into the fussy-cut foreground details such as flowers right away. If you work on them first, however, you will have to pick them up again when you need to position other parts of your landscape behind them. Be patient and *always work forward from whatever is farthest away.*

As you work, you will quickly discover that the quilt batting is fibrous. Your fabric will stick to it without the necessity of fusing or glue, so if something is not working for you, it will be very easy to pick up that fabric piece and replace it with something else. You don't need to pin anything down. The pins will just get in your way later when it is time to place the final tulle layer on your quilt.

Don't rush. Enjoy the process: Experiment and analyze. Give the fabric a chance to speak to you! For example, if you are using a batik, maybe something in the pattern will suggest fluffy bushes or tree foliage. Keep your eyes open for inspiration from your fabric!

DEALING WITH SHREDDING FABRICS

Another thing to consider is how tightly or loosely woven a particular piece of fabric is. I use a lot of batiks because, unlike most printed fabrics, they don't shred very easily.

If you are doing a lot of fussy cutting on printed fabric that tends to shred, you will probably want to fuse it. But don't get too concerned about a bit of shredding. Once you start stitching over the tulle, you will soon discover that a few random shreds can be coaxed back under a fabric edge by poking them out of sight with a pin. The stitching will keep them from escaping.

You may even want to take advantage of your fabric's shredding tendencies. For example, skies can be especially tricky, and your fabric can help or hinder your efforts to recreate it in an effective way. When we look at a sky photograph or an actual sky, we often fail to recognize how softly and subtly the various colors, even the brightest ones, blend together and how most clouds have soft, wispy edges.

One of my students solved this problem very effectively. She purposely tore strips of blue, gray, pale pink, and light yellow fabric and overlapped them. Laying them across her batting and allowing their frayed edges to merge, she suggested the misty expanse of a moody sky. Water in a bay, ocean, lake, or river could be dealt with in much the same way.

On the other hand, if you look at mid-twentieth century posters that advertise travel to our national parks, many of them are done in a style that treats everything in the landscape, including the clouds, with hard edges. Several students have shown that this can be quite effective if carried throughout the entire quilt.

TO FUSE OR NOT TO FUSE?

Feel free to fuse and glue if it makes you feel more secure. But be aware that this will limit your ability to revise your fabric choices and to easily add or remove design elements. When I am working on a quilt that includes many small pieces of fabric, such as windows on a building, I do use glue or a fusible. I don't want to sneeze and have tiny windows flying all over my studio!

A REMINDER ABOUT TAKING PHOTOS

Because you are working flat on a table, rather than on a design wall, it can be really difficult to assess the overall visual effect of your landscape (not to mention how tired your back can become!). As you continue to work, be sure that you periodically take a break and snap a photo of your work to get an entirely different perspective on your creation. This is an easy way to view your quilt on your phone or camera exactly as you will be seeing it once it is hanging on your wall.

 Tip To avoid distortion or a strange perspective of your project, you will need to carefully position your phone or camera as horizontally as possible over your project before you snap your picture!

THE FOREGROUND

The last step in creating your landscape is to develop the foreground.

When one of my Asilomar students reached this point in his Japanese garden quilt project, which included a pond, a rather elaborate Japanese teahouse, and several geishas, he came to me for help. "I'm stumped, Meri. I don't think I can figure out how to construct that teahouse. It seems very complicated."

Fortunately, it turned out that the picture he had brought to class was printed on high-quality rice paper. "Why don't you just cut out the teahouse and insert it into your landscape?" I suggested. It worked like a charm! He cut out the teahouse and also took his scissors to the geishas. Once he had added his final layer of tulle, he was able to stitch right around and over those elements. The end result was a lovely Japanese-inspired quilt!

This is the time to have fun using all those great soft embellishments like lace, trim, yarn, and fussy-cut flowers, leaves, and plants that you have been itching to add to your quilt! It is also your opportunity to capture the attention of your viewer and encourage him or her to step in for a closer look. The elements you choose for your foreground will give your landscape life and vitality!

Detail of foreground ferns and roses in *Arlington Row in Bibury Village, the Cotswolds, England* (See full quilt, page 26.)

NOTE: Do not *add any hard embellishments such as beads right now because they will distort the final tulle layer. You will almost certainly break your needle when you try to quilt around or over them. All hard embellishments should be added* after *you have quilted your quilt!*

THE FINAL TULLE LAYER

Once you have completed your landscape to your satisfaction, it is time to apply your final layer of tulle.

Tulle comes in an amazing variety of colors. *Be sure to only use fine-mesh tulle*; you want the tulle to disappear into the quilt and not call attention to itself. Viewers are always amazed when you point out that there is black tulle covering your entire picture!

You will definitely want to purchase some fine black tulle; for some reason, it is usually the best choice for most quilts. Surprisingly, it seems to make colors appear richer instead of duller. Another very useful color is navy blue for shadows. It will help nail down objects and people in your quilt so they don't appear to be floating off the ground. I also use various shades of pink to push parts of my landscapes into the distance. A rosy-pink tulle, rather than black, works great as a final overall layer because it can lend a romantic tint to your landscape under the right circumstances.

Grand Canyon Sunset (page 22) presented several interesting challenges. A beautiful photograph on the cover of *Sunset* magazine inspired me. Well, actually, it *insisted* that I had to make this quilt! The image was vertical, however, and I wanted to create a horizontal landscape that would encompass the great panoramic expanse of the canyon vista. This meant that I had to invent the areas to the right and left of the central section of my quilt. Several hours of research on my trusty laptop gave me a good sense of what the canyon looked like in general and how sunlight and shadow affected the colors of the rocks at different times of the day. With this information in mind, I was able to fill in the blanks with wedges of striped batiks and a gleam of dupioni silk to represent a glimpse of the Colorado River winding through the canyon below.

Detail of batik cliff walls and Dupioni silk river in *Grand Canyon Sunset* (See full quilt, page 22.)

Further complications arose when I was unable to find fabric that represented the moody evening sky, so I was forced to paint it. When I tried to put black tulle over the entire landscape, it was obvious that it killed the vibrant ambiance of the canyon, especially the hand-painted sky. I ended up leaving the sky uncovered and placed light pink tulle only over the canyon itself. Then I hand appliquéd the foreground ledges over the pink tulle and canyon to make them appear closer to the viewer.

Rosy-pink tulle was also the perfect choice for *Arlington Row in Bibury Village, the Cotswolds, England* (page 26), a place that has great sentimental value for me.

Years ago, when I was writing my first science fiction story, I needed to imagine a place that my characters could call home. A photograph in *Sunset* magazine's travel section really grabbed my attention. Although I had no idea where that place was—except that it was in England—I pinned it up on my wall next to my old typewriter, and thus it became Valhalla in my story. Flash forward to 2010, when I was visiting England with some friends. We drove around a corner in a very famous area called the Cotswolds, and there it was! I dashed out of the car and began snapping pictures like mad. These pictures inspired the quilt you see today.

My photograph of Arlington Row, Bibury Village, the Cotswolds, England   *Photo by Meri Henriques Vahl*

Grand Canyon Sunset, 49″ × 32″, by Meri Henriques Vahl

I began with the sky, which is the most distant part of the scene, and then used batiks and various Stonehenge fabrics for most of the background foliage and shrubbery.

Detail of trees and sky in *Arlington Row in Bibury Village, the Cotswolds, England* (See full quilt, page 26.)

Next, I created the most distant row of cottages using my Paper Doll Technique (page 64), which I will explain in detail later.

Detail of cottages in *Arlington Row in Bibury Village, the Cotswolds, England* (See full quilt, page 26.)

When I started working into the foreground, many of the printed flowers, especially the individual roses that I wanted to collage into bushes, needed to be fused to prevent them from shredding.

When it was finally time to audition an overlying layer of tulle, the black tulle was a disaster! My beloved Arlington Row scene suddenly looked very gloomy indeed, and it was obvious that I needed to pick a different color. Pink turned out to be the ideal choice for a romantic scene, surrounded by a border of hand-appliquéd and beaded roses and vines.

Detail of rose bushes in *Arlington Row in Bibury Village, the Cotswolds, England* (See full quilt, page 26.)

Detail of right-hand border in *Arlington Row in Bibury Village, the Cotswolds, England* (See full quilt, page 26.)

Arlington Row in Bibury Village, the Cotswolds, England, 46″ × 32″, by Meri Henriques Vahl

When you are choosing which tulle to use to cover your landscape, it is often a good idea to try a couple of different colors. Make sure that you have ironed out those pesky and inevitable wrinkles first! Be sure to use an iron set on cool or iron with a piece of fabric placed over the tulle. Tulle is synthetic and therefore quite easy to melt, so *don't set your hot iron directly on it*!

Get a friend to help you carefully place the tulle over your landscape so you don't accidentally shift the collage pieces that you have worked so hard to set in place. And make sure you haven't left in any of those pins (you know—the ones you didn't really need to use in your picture!).

 *Tip* If you do leave a pin in your quilt, don't panic! I once did just that and didn't discover the hidden pin until I began to stitch. I was in a panic until my very practical friend Ellen Edith suggested that I smash the buried glass pinhead with a hammer, after which I was able to easily work the metal pin shaft out of the quilt.

PINNING YOUR QUILT

Once your tulle is in place, it's time to get out those pins! Don't be stingy—put in as many pins as you need to keep your fabric pieces and soft embellishments from shifting around while you are quilting your project.

 Tip Since I grab hold of my quilt while I am stitching it, I can't use straight pins without risking getting bloodstains on my project. I like to use Wrights 670160 Basting Brights Safety Pins because they have a very thin shaft, a very sharp point, and they won't poke big holes in my quilt—or in me!

No matter what kind of pins you use, either straight or safety, be sure to stagger them! If you line them up one right above the other, you will discover that your quilt has developed waves. This will make it difficult to get it to lie nice and flat while you are stitching and even afterward.

Inspired by a Galen Rowell photograph, *Pink Sunset* is a quilt that I had intended use as a class sample and send off to quilt guilds to advertise my upcoming classes. When I reached the pinning stage of the quilt and before I had a chance to stitch it, my students begged me to leave it as is, pins and all. They wanted to see just how many pins I had added (lots, even for this small quilt!) and how I had arranged them across the quilt surface. Those pins would have been removed as I stitched, but I guess now that will never happen!

QUILTING

It's time to start quilting! The wonderful thing about this technique is that every stitch you make now will be trapping the fabric pieces, yarn, and fussy-cut elements under the tulle so they won't have a chance to move around. At the same time, you will be quilting your landscape! This will save you lots of time. You don't need to make a traditional quilt top, which then must be placed on top of batting and a quilt backing before stitching all the separate elements together.

Set up your sewing machine for free-motion quilting. Be sure to insert a topstitch needle; it has a longer eye and will help prevent skipped stitches. Lower your feed dogs and upper tension. I prefer to use 100% cotton thread, but polyester is also fine—it just depends on what you like and what you have in your stash.

In order to create the least distortion possible, *start quilting in the middle of your landscape*, and work outward from there, removing pins as you go.

Pinned *Pink Sunset*, approximately 19½˝ × 26˝, by Meri Henriques Vahl

Whenever you are stitching an object, such as a mountain or a tree, *do not* start by outlining it. Instead, do some stitching inside the object itself to nail it down first. Otherwise, because tulle itself is a bit slippery, you will soon make the unhappy discovery that your tree, mountain, or person has shifted slightly, which will result in a lovely line of perfect stitching that's about ¹⁄₁₆″ away from the edge of your object!

Detail of basket maker in *The Basket Makers of Axoum, Ethiopia* (See full quilt, page 84.)

PREPARING YOUR LANDSCAPE FOR BORDERS

Now that you have quilted your landscape, it is time to steam and iron it flat. Make sure you turn your iron setting down to cool or place a protective cloth layer over the tulle to keep it from melting and ruining both your quilt and your iron!

Allow your quilt to cool down, dry, and set. Now you're ready to square it up (which I will discuss in A Simple Landscape Collage, page 44)! I will show you how to put the finishing touches on your project in Finishing Your Quilt: Borders, Binding, and More! (page 96).

Some Design Considerations

Let's talk about design. Whether it is a painting or an art quilt, a well-designed picture should welcome the viewer in and encourage him or her to stay awhile and take a look around.

Perhaps you have seen a painting or quilt that portrays a vase of flowers set smack in the middle of the picture or a horizon line in a landscape that cuts the image exactly in half from top to bottom. This is a static picture: Once you have taken your first look, your eye has nowhere else to go. You will probably lose interest and move on to the next quilt or painting.

It would be a much more interesting composition if some of the leaves and flowers went all the way out to the edges of the quilt or spilled over onto the border. Interest could also be added by placing the back edge of the table either above or below the middle of the quilt and moving the vase slightly off-center. Perhaps a butterfly or a line of bees are entering the picture, some still partway in the border and heading towards a flower. You can bet the viewer's eyes will follow that!

VISUAL IMPACT

It is important for your landscape to have a visual impact from a distance and draw the viewer closer to check out the details. There are many ways to do this: through the use of color, pattern, or perspective, or even a literal path that says to the viewer, "Come closer and step into my world."

Many of my quilts have an actual path that starts at the front edge of the landscape and recedes into the picture. For example, both *Arlington Row in Bibury Village, the Cotswolds, England* (page 26) and *Free Tibet* (page 36) include this element.

Path detail in *Free Tibet* (See full quilt, page 36.)

Creating Visual Movement Through Texture and Color

Texture—both visual and tactile—also creates movement. For example, the ridges in corduroy or the linear or swirling patterns in fabric can be effectively used to encourage the viewer to explore your landscape.

Detail of textured and patterned mountain fabric in *Free Tibet* (See full quilt, page 36.)

For the more distant landscape elements, be sure to use fabric that suggests distance. In other words, it is probably not a good idea to put something bright with a large, bold pattern in the far background, because it will appear to jump forward into the foreground and confuse the viewer.

As you get closer to the foreground, have fun! Start including those larger, patterned fabrics and perhaps add yarn and fussy-cut flowers to suggest close-up grass or plants.

Color is another useful device that can lead the viewer's eye around a landscape or picture. For example, a series of items (like bright flowers, autumn trees, green bushes, or cacti in a tan desert setting) that are scattered throughout your landscape will encourage the viewer to look at all the different aspects of your quilt. It will be sure to keep their interest.

Using Perspective and Size to Create Visual Movement

You can also create visual movement in your quilts through the use of perspective. If you start with small design elements in the distance and gradually increase their size as you approach the foreground, you will add a great deal of interest to your quilt. A street that is lined with buildings and telephone poles appears to be narrower and smaller the farther away it is from you. By varying the sizes of the objects in your quilt, you can get the same effect. If you analyze the photograph you have chosen to work with, you will readily see that this is also true in nature.

For example, foreground leaves should appear to be larger and more detailed than foliage that is further back. Buildings in the foreground look bigger than distant buildings. Be sure to think about this as you select your fabrics and take advantage of the scale—the amount of pattern and detail—that you choose for the different layers of your project.

You can see all of these elements and visual techniques at work in my quilt, *Arlington Row in Bibury Village, the Cotswolds, England* (page 26).

Detail of cottages receding into distance in *Arlington Row in Bibury Village, the Cotswolds, England* (See full quilt, page 26.)

Detail of celebrating people in *Free Tibet* (See full quilt, page 36.)

Free Tibet was inspired by my respect for His Holiness the Dalai Lama, from my years' long fascination with the Tibetan people and landscapes, and by Galen Rowell's photographs of the Himalaya Mountains. In my imagination, I fantasized that if the Dalai Lama was ever able to return to his lost homeland, the local people would all joyfully come out to greet him.

Detail of yarn yak and women in *Free Tibet* (See full quilt, page 36.)

Each of the people, the yak, and the two palaces were constructed with the same Paper Doll Technique (page 64). As for the rest of the landscape, I invented that myself based upon what I had previously viewed during my virtual tours.

Once the black tulle layer had been stitched over the people and landscape, I added all the beading and appliquéd the two trumpet players on top of the tulle and partway onto the border so they would appear to be closer to the viewer.

Detail of trumpet player in *Free Tibet* (See full quilt, page 36.)

Free Tibet, 72″ × 49″, by Meri Henriques Vahl

I was thrilled when *Free Tibet* earned me my third grand prize at the Mancuso Brothers Best Quilts of the World contest in 2015!

More Design Considerations

Here are some other things to think about.

It is useful to remember that the farther away something is from the viewer (such as a distant mountain range), the paler it is. So take advantage of those softer colors and gradually shade toward bolder and brighter foreground fabrics!

Printed fabric has two sides: a brighter front and a much lighter back. You can create some great effects by using the reverse side of your printed fabric. You can achieve a more distant look or even the effects of light and shadow.

You can incorporate any type of fabric into your quilt that you can stitch over. Corduroy, denim, seersucker (like the more distant roofs in *Arlington Row in Bibury Village, the Cotswolds, England*, page 26), or textured velvet are all options. What you end up using depends on the look you want to create.

The mountain fabric in *Beyond the Blue Mountains* (page 15) is somewhat of an exception. It works because it shades from light to dark and has a subtle print that doesn't call too much attention to itself. Instead, it suggests faraway texture and linear movement, which pulls the mountains together as a whole visual unit.

Mountain detail in *Beyond the Blue Mountains* (See full quilt, page 15.)

ADDING SOFT EMBELLISHMENTS

This is also the time to think about the interesting soft embellishments that can be placed on the quilt before you cover it with the final tulle layer.

Wool roving or cotton from a pill bottle can be pulled and stretched out to make soft fluffy clouds, as can been seen in the sky in *Free Tibet*.

Detail of wool roving as clouds in *Free Tibet* (See full quilt, page 36.)

A couple of pieces of dark blue yarn added interest to the sky in *The Grand Tetons* (page 42), and the closer hills in *Beyond the Blue Mountains* (page 15) are embellished with strips of fuzzy olive-green selvage, which I cut from the pleated olive-green fabric that was used for the mid-distance hills.

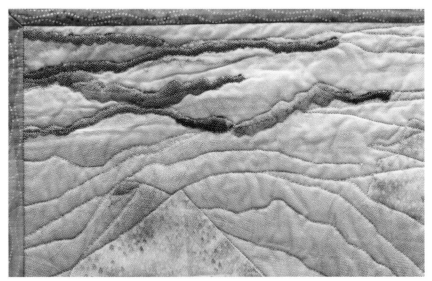

Detail of yarn in the sky in *The Grand Tetons* (See full quilt, page 42.)

Detail of the close hills in *Beyond the Blue Mountains* (See full quilt, page 15.)

Cheesecloth can be teased, folded, and stretched out to create fantastic frothy ocean waves. Lace can suggest lovely curtains or ornate wooden trim on an old building. Paper, real leaves, and feathers are also fair game. If you like the effect any particular item lends to your quilt, by all means, put it in!

All those thread ends you cut off the front of your sewing machine rather than pulling them back through it when you were changing thread colors are a hidden treasure. They can be scattered across your landscape to suggest grass, thin forest branches, or shrubs.

In other words, don't throw anything away. Collage quilts will give you a marvelous excuse for collecting even more stuff than you already have!

ENHANCING YOUR LANDSCAPE WITH STITCHING

Stitching can add a whole lot of visual interest and detail to your quilt. It is also the design element that physically holds your quilt together, so be sure to take advantage of this!

Taking another look at my *Arlington Row in Bibury Village* quilt. You'll see that I did extensive stitching on the closer cottage tile roofs and also on the trees, flower beds, and rose bushes. This quilt has more thread work on it than any of my large quilts!

Detail of roof stitching in *Arlington Row in Bibury Village, the Cotswolds, England* (See full quilt, page 26.)

In *Hawking's Bubbles II: e = mc²*, each "bubble" consists of just five or six wedges of overlapping batik fabrics that were secured in place by a few colorful wavy lines of stitching. All the beading, like the twisted bugle beads and other decorative glass beads, was applied afterward. The original version of this quilt, which was inspired by a photograph of soap bubbles in Dr. Stephen Hawking's *The Illustrated a Brief History of Time*, was made as a much larger and sort of futuristic three-dimensional crazy quilt with heavily padded bubbles that featured a "black hole" in the center of each one. Even as I was constructing it—which was a real feat of engineering—I thought it would be quite interesting to try to recreate it in two dimensions. So when I was asked to participate in a challenge with restricted dimensions and the requirement that the quilt must contain at least one word (I was allowed to get away with "e = mc²"), it seemed like the perfect excuse to do so!

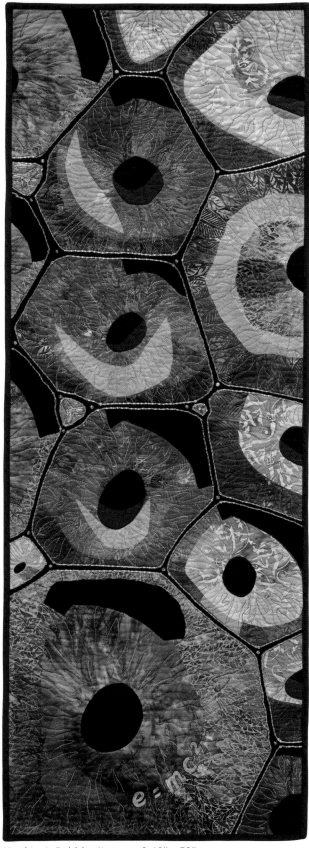

Hawking's Bubbles II: e = mc², 18″ × 52″, by Meri Henriques Vahl

Detail of yarn grass foreground in *The Grand Tetons* (See full quilt, below.)

Now, take a close look at *The Grand Tetons*. The grassy knoll in the foreground was created by laying down a piece of light brown batik and tossing short pieces of yarn and fussy-cut flowers onto it.

The Grand Tetons, 34″ × 27″, by Meri Henriques Vahl

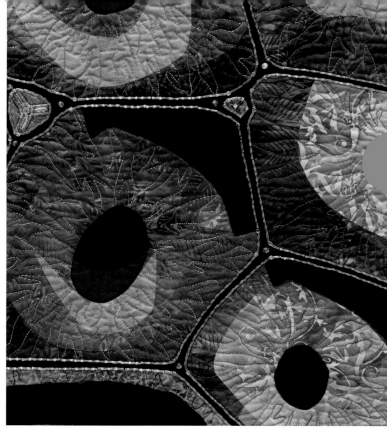

When it came time to machine quilt *The Grand Tetons*, I randomly stitched some wavy up-and-down lines over the tulle, similar to the technique I used in *Hawking's Bubbles II: e = mc²*. That's all it took to keep the yarn in place!

Detail of random wavy stitching on bubble in *Hawking's Bubbles II: e = mc²* (See full quilt, page 41.)

Detail of pine tree needle stitching in *The Grand Tetons* (See full quilt, previous page.)

I also did quite a lot of stitching on the fussy-cut clumps of pine needles, taking advantage of the bright green thread that gives them a spiky look and adds some richer color to the pine tree foliage. You might want to think about this when you are trying to decide on thread colors for your own quilt.

Tip Remember: If you are adding beaded embellishments, such as any of the glittering leaflike beads in my *The Grand Tetons* quilt, be sure to add them *after* you have finished stitching your quilt so you won't break your needle when you try to sew over them!

A Simple Landscape Collage

Although I encourage students to choose their own landscape photograph for their first collage quilt, you will find a simple landscape project that you can make using one of my own personal photographs of the Grand Tetons in Wyoming. Whether or not you decide to work with my photo, the actual size you make the central image of your quilt is entirely up to you.

Before you begin your project, please read through the entire instructions to decide on the approximate amounts of fabrics you may want to use. Your choices will depend on how big you want the landscape part of your quilt to be. Remember: There are no rules! Please feel free to improvise as you go with fabric choices, as with anything else. Refer to Some Design Considerations (page 31) for specific ideas about ways to design your quilt.

Think about what size you would like your final quilt to be *minus the borders*. Then select fabric for your quilt backing and batting that is just a bit larger, with maybe an extra 1″ or 2″ on all sides. This will give you plenty of area to play with.

Grand Tetons *Photo by Meri Henriques Vahl*

Please note that, by necessity, the fabrics you select will be different from the ones I have used—your quilt will not be an exact duplicate of mine. It will be fun to see how similar yet different our two versions of the same photograph will turn out to be!

MATERIALS

- Nice landscape photo (Or see my Grand Tetons photo, above.)

- Selection of fabrics, such as batiks, cotton prints, silk, velvet, and corduroy

- Fabric for your quilt backing, approximately 30″ × 22″ (or any size you wish)

- Batting, approximately the same size as the backing

- Fine-mesh tulle in various colors (black, navy blue, rose, and so on)

- *Lots* of pins (I like Wrights Basting Brights Safety Pins, but straight pins are also fine.)

- Topstitch needles for your sewing machine

- *Optional:* Soft embellishments that can be stitched over, such as yarn, roving, cheesecloth, lace, and ribbon

Grand Tetons Revisited, 20¼″ × 28″, by Meri Henriques Vahl

1 BEGINNING THE LANDSCAPE

Iron the fabric you have chosen for your quilt back. Place it *facedown* on your worktable.

Don't worry about leaving enough extra quilt back and batting for the borders. Right now you will just be working on the landscape section of the quilt. Once you have finished stitching your quilt, you will square it up. I will teach you how to add borders, binding, or even more quilt in Finishing Your Quilt: Borders, Binding, and More! (page 96).

Place a piece of batting that is more or less the same size as your quilt back right on top of it on your worktable, as described in The Fabric Collage with Tulle Overlay Technique (page 15).

2 CHOOSING AND ENHANCING THE SKY

Begin your landscape with whatever is farthest away: in this case, the sky. Audition sky fabric to find which one pleases you the most. Just keep in mind that you might want to change this fabric later once you see how it works with the other fabrics you have chosen.

While you are trying to decide what sky fabric to use, you may also want to audition fabric for other parts of the landscape, such as the mountains, trees, and river, to see how your various choices will look together.

NOTE: *One of the many great things about this technique is that nothing is nailed down. This will allow you to revise your picture, if needed, as you go along.*

You can make your landscape as simple or as elaborate as you wish. You are not trying to recreate the photograph; what you *are* doing is trying to express your own personal feelings about a particular place. Once you feel satisfied with your sky and are auditioning mountain fabrics, you may want to switch to a different sky fabric that works better with your mountains.

Iron the sky fabric you have chosen and place it directly on the batting. A few strands of yarn, some navy-blue tulle, fluffed-out aspirin bottle cotton, roving (which is what I chose to use for my version of *Grand Tetons Revisited*), or white tulle can be added to represent the clouds. On the other hand, you can omit the clouds altogether. It's entirely up to you!

 Tip Think in overlapping layers! Be sure to leave enough extra fabric on the bottom edge of your sky so the next layer you put down (the mountains) will overlap and cover up the bottom edge of the sky layer.

Carefully ironed sky fabric on batting; cloud detail created with white roving

3 AUDITIONING MOUNTAIN FABRIC AND CUTTING OUT MOUNTAINS

If you have not already done so, this is the time to start auditioning mountain fabric. Choose something that works well against the sky fabric you have chosen. The mountain fabric should probably have some visual or tactile texture—for example, corduroy—so you can play with alternating the direction of the fabric ridges. The ridges can suggest alternating rock bed layers and create visual movement. Whatever fabric you choose, be sure its pattern is not so large that it will overshadow and dominate your foreground when you add it later on!

Once you have made your decision, have fun cutting out a couple of jagged mountain peaks. For this quilt, I have cut the mountains in several different pieces: the largest central peak and the smaller ones in front and on either side.

 Tip If you prefer, you can draw and cut out freezer-paper pattern pieces, but it's also interesting to go along with whatever the fabric's texture or pattern suggests and to make the cuts it inspires you to choose. Your mountains don't have to exactly duplicate what you see in the photograph.

Place the mountains right over the sky. Make sure you have left an extra margin of fabric along the bottom mountain edge; this will be covered by the next layer of fabric. If you have used some white tulle, roving, or cotton for the clouds, you might want to lay some more of it over parts of the mountains to create a soft, hazy look.

Hand-cut mountain peaks placed over sky

4 DESIGNING THE RIVER

By *carefully analyzing* my photograph and the finished quilt, you will quickly notice that the river extends from the far distance right up to the foreground. I think of it as a sort of visual path that will lead the viewer into the scene. Every other element of the landscape—whether it is the shorelines (from the most distant to the closest), the trees, or the grassy hill in the foreground—is easier to work with if you first place a big chunk of water fabric down *before* you add those other elements.

So get out your fabric stash and start auditioning river fabric! Choose something slightly darker than the sky but lighter than the mountains—maybe even a striped batik. Since there are no rules, your favorite fabric may be something entirely different, like leaping dolphins or a solid.

Whatever fabric you choose, cut out the river and place it on your batting, making sure that it overlaps the bottom edge of the mountains.

This might be a good time to take a picture, holding your camera or phone horizontally over your quilt. This will give you a good idea of how the various elements of your picture are starting to work together. Remember: Unless you take a photo, you don't really have an accurate perspective on how the finished quilt is going to look when you hang it up on your wall because you are designing flat on your worktable.

Some possible river fabrics and my final choice

5 THE DISTANT RIVER SHORE

Start with the distant river shore. Cut and lay a strip of fabric along the top of the river, being sure to overlap it on the water fabric.

Batik fabrics come in a wide range of patterns and styles. Batiks with softly painted stripes are especially good for landscape work, and I always grab a yard or two whenever I encounter some in a fabric store or quilt show. But any fabric that works for you is just fine, too.

Instead of a batik or other fabric, you can add yarn or a strip of fancy ribbon to suggest the distant forest. Or perhaps you will cut your distant river-shore fabric strip with a jagged upper edge to get the same effect!

Distant river shore

6 | THE CLOSER RIVER-SHORE EDGES

Now you can begin to construct the closer river-shore edges the same way. Choose the fabric you would like to use for the land along the shoreline in the middle distance. Some more of that lovely striped batik from another part of the same yardage might just do the trick!

It's also time to start thinking about the trees. The ones on the left-hand river shore are closer and therefore larger than the ones on the right side of the river, so you can either find printed fabric that has trees of different sizes or you can fussy cut some.

I used an interesting spotted batik fabric for the more distant trees and let the patterns in the fabric suggest where to cut rounded foliage shapes. When I was ready to stitch them, I added even more foliage shapes with my thread.

Then I chose a printed fabric for the closer trees to add more detail and to make them appear closer to the viewer. Since this was a more loosely woven fabric, it was important to iron fusible onto the back before I began cutting around the tree shapes. This was the only part of the project that required the application of a fusible. Every other element of the landscape, including the yarn in the foreground, was laid directly on the quilt without the necessity of any kind of glue or fusible.

If you use printed fabric on any part of your quilt, you will probably want to iron some fusible to the back of the fabric to prevent the edges from fraying. Since printed fabric has two sides, consider cutting some of the trees from the right side of the fabric and some from the wrong side to add interest and suggest the interplay of light and shadow on the foliage.

 Tip It might be a good time to take another photo to see how your quilt is coming along.

Closer river-shore edges and trees

7 THE FOREGROUND

Foregrounds are fun! Let your imagination run wild. You can do as much fussy cutting and embellishment as you like, perhaps adding some fussy-cut flowers and yarn, or pieces of thread to suggest grass (that's how I dealt with the foreground in this *Grand Tetons Revisited* quilt). If you have the perfect fabric that says it all, go ahead and use it!

Feel free to omit the pine tree in the foreground if you decide that it is either too complicated or doesn't add interest to your quilt.

NOTE: *This is not the time to add beads or any other hard materials to your quilt. They will distort the final tulle layer and will probably break your sewing machine needle when you try to stitch your project!*

When I took the photograph that inspired this quilt, I was standing on a grassy riverbank; however, when it came time to work on my original *The Grand Tetons* (page 42) foreground, I could not find fabric that represented what I had seen there. To solve the problem, I chose a brown batik with a subtle pattern. I cut and threw down many strands of various colored and textured yarns, plus fussy-cut flowers. There was no need to glue down any of the yarn to keep it in place until I could stitch the quilt. But I was careful to disturb it as little as possible until I placed the black tulle over the entire quilt in preparation for stitching. I dealt with the *Grand Tetons Revisited* (page 45) foreground in the same way. You can do the same or invent your own solution.

Now that you've finished constructing your landscape, take another photograph to make sure you are satisfied with the way it has come together. Decide if you need to change anything—add or subtract any details, substitute a different fabric somewhere, or reposition a design element. You can always change things later after you have chosen and set down your tulle layer but *before* you pin the tulle down; it is your best and easiest chance to do so.

Foreground with fabric added

8   AUDITIONING THE FINAL TULLE LAYER

Stitching over the tulle is what will hold your quilt together, so the next step in making your landscape is to decide what color your final tulle layer will be.

Lighter colors of tulle, such as light blue, beige, and white, will usually obscure your picture and make it look dull, taking all the vibrancy and life out of it. However, there are a few unique occasions when light-colored tulle is exactly what is called for. When one of my students made a lovely landscape of the moon rising over a Chinese lake, black tulle made it look like something out of *Dracula*. A final layer of silvery tulle came to the rescue, infusing her entire quilt with a soft, moonlit glow and turning it into a real showpiece. The moral of the story is don't take anything for granted, be willing to experiment, and stand back (or photograph) to analyze the results.

That silver tulle was an exception. Surprisingly, very fine black tulle is usually the best solution for most quilts. It somehow enriches the colors rather than dulling them down. I recommend that you start by auditioning black tulle. If it sucks all the life and color out of your quilt, try another color.

Tulle has a way of developing subtle waves and wrinkles. Before you try to set it down on your quilt, lay it flat on an ironing surface, place a large piece of fabric over it, and iron it really carefully, making sure you don't melt it. Alternatively, you can turn your iron's setting down to cool and iron directly on your tulle. But keep in mind that tulle is made from a plastic-like synthetic that can easily melt and ruin your iron as well as all of your hard work. I always stay on the safe side and iron my tulle using a warm setting with a protective cover cloth over it.

Get a friend to help you very carefully place your tulle over your quilt. Check out the effect and take a picture if you have any doubts. If black tulle doesn't look good on your quilt, another possible choice is rosy-pink tulle. This is what I used for *Arlington Row in Bibury Village, the Cotswolds, England* (page 26). The pink tulle gave the scene a nice, soft romantic look that black tulle just couldn't provide.

9   PINNING THE LANDSCAPE

It's time to start pinning! Be sure to use *lots* of pins. Pins are very important in this step because they are what will hold your quilt together while you are stitching.

NOTE: *I use Wright's Basting Brights. They have very thin shanks and very sharp points, and they don't poke big holes in my fabric. Depending on how you like to free-motion quilt, you can use straight pins or whatever you prefer.*

Keep smoothing out the tulle as you apply your pins, and be sure you stagger them across the quilt surface. If you line up your pins one right above the other, they will end up creating waves in your quilt. It will be very difficult to get your quilt to lie nice and flat while you are stitching and even afterward.

Now that your tulle is pinned in place, you can pick up your quilt and put it up on your design wall. If there is something you aren't happy with, carefully remove some of the pins, turn back the tulle, and fix whatever is bothering you.

If some element has shifted a bit in the process, you may be able to gently poke it back into place with a straight pin rather than lifting up part of the tulle. Make sure you don't distort or rip the tulle in the process!

Two possible tulle choices and quilt with final black tulle layer placed over it and pinned

QUILTING

Your quilt is ready for stitching! To set your sewing machine up for free-motion quilting, lower the feed dogs and decrease the upper tension so the bobbin thread won't show on the surface of your quilt.

Before you start quilting, insert a topstitch needle in your sewing machine. Topstitch needles have a longer eye, which helps prevent your machine from skipping stitches while you are sewing through multiple layers of fabric.

Start quilting in the center of your quilt and move outward toward the edges, removing pins as you go. If the tulle shifts or develops waves while you are stitching, remove some of the pins in that area, smooth out the renegade tulle, and pin it back down again.

Stitching can add a great deal of interest to your quilt. Take your time to evaluate what kind of stitching and thread colors will best enhance the elements of your landscape. For example, while stitching wavy horizontal lines across your river, keep the lines that are farthest away close together and increase the spacing between them as you get closer and closer to the foreground. By doing this, you will be adding perspective to your scene.

On the other hand, if you don't want your stitching to be a design element in your quilt, you can use neutral-color thread or thread that closely matches the fabric you are going to stitch on. However, I advocate courage. Allow the thread to give new dimension, texture, and color to your project. It sometimes takes me several attempts and do-overs, not to mention the careful use of a seam ripper, before I am able to find exactly the right thread for any given part of my quilt.

Whenever you encounter an object, such as a tree, flower, or mountain, *stitch first in the center of it*. If you outline it first before adding interior stitching, you will be very unhappy when you discover that the edges of your tree or mountain have crept away from your carefully stitched outlines!

Look closely at the yarn in the foreground of my quilt. I did not have to sew down every single strand of yarn; some random wavy lines of stitching held everything in place, and the yarn stayed where I placed it. You can see this even better if you look at the back of the quilt.

Foreground detail with yarn added, quilt front

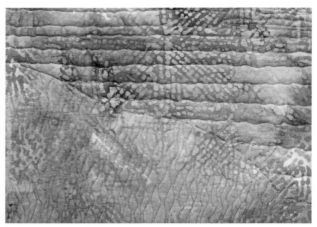

Foreground detail, quilt back

When you have finished stitching, carefully steam the quilt flat, remembering to protect the front of the quilt so you don't melt the tulle with the hot iron when you do so. Allow it to dry thoroughly.

Stitched and steamed *Grand Tetons Revisited* landscape

SQUARING UP YOUR LANDSCAPE

Once your quilt is dry and lies nice and flat, you will need to square it up. Use a cutting mat and rulers to ensure accuracy. A large 12½″ square ruler and a rotary chalk marking tool are very helpful for this purpose. If your quilt measures the same diagonally from corner to corner in both directions after you have made your cuts, you know you have done the job right!

To complete your quilt, see Finishing Your Quilt: Borders, Binding, and More! (page 96).

NOTE: *Although it is tempting to add hard embellishments such as beads now to give your foreground that added sparkle and make it appear even closer to the viewer, it is best to wait until you have completed your borders to do so.*

Squared-up quilt, 24½" × 16½"

The Paper Doll Technique

At first glance, everyone is intimidated by the prospect of putting people into a quilt. That is because the human form is so familiar to us that we can't help wanting our person to be perfect.

Of course, you can always use a photo transfer, but to my eye, the photo transfer of a person is always quite obvious. The person looks rather dull and fails to blend in well with the more vivid colors and fabric in the rest of the quilt. The only time that I have personally seen an effective photo transfer was when one of my Asilomar students transferred her people onto silk fabric. The silk gave depth and more vibrant color to their faces, skin tones, and clothing than a transfer onto cotton fabric would have been able to achieve.

So maybe it's time to try a different approach to people. Be brave! I promise that if you can trace a line, I can teach you how to create people my way!

You are now familiar with the Fabric Collage with Tulle Overlay Technique, and you have completed your landscape (you can think of it as a stage for your people). *Before you apply that final layer of tulle*, consider adding a person or several people to your quilt. This is where the Paper Doll Technique comes in. I think of this technique as playing with paper dolls, and it is the same technique I use to create all the buildings, animals, furniture, and other items I can "build" separately and add to my quilt. The Paper Doll Technique gives me the freedom to move a person or object around within the quilt area until I am completely satisfied with its placement. Let's begin!

In order to teach you how you make people my way, I will now show you with step-by-step photos how I created Rosa for my *Flower Market* quilt. You can follow these same steps when you create your own person. The *Flower Market at Chichicastenango, Guatemala*, presented many other interesting creative challenges, not the least of which was choosing the right people.

Flower Market at Chichicastenango, Guatemala, 64″ × 46″, by Meri Henriques Vahl

Detail of Rosa in *Flower Market at Chichicastenango, Guatemala* (See full quilt, page 64.)

A VERY IMPORTANT NOTE: *You must take this process slowly. It is imperative that you* carefully and constantly observe and analyze *your color and black-and-white photographs as you proceed!*

MATERIALS

- Color photo of person you want to create

- Black-and-white copy of your person on *plain* (*not* glossy) *paper*, in the *exact size* you want him or her to be in your finished quilt

- Lightbox or bright window

- Fabric for clothing, so you can dress your person

- Fine- and medium-point permanent markers, especially black and brown

- Freezer paper

- Good-quality colored pencils in dark blue, white, and black, and in colors to match your person's skin tone: light blue, rose red, yellow, brown, tan, and so on (I like to use Caran d'Ache watercolor pencils, but any good-quality colored pencils will be just fine.)

- Spray fixative (I use Matte Finish 1311 by Krylon, which is usually used for pastel chalk drawings and can be found in any art supply or craft store.)

- Paper-backed fusible webbing (I like Lite Steam-A-Seam 2 or other paper-backed fusible that has a smooth surface—*not* dots of glue, which can make your person's skin look like it has a rash!)

- Medium-weight fusible interfacing (I use 808 Craft-Fuse by Pellon. It has a smooth glue surface, *not* dots of glue.)

- Tightly-woven cotton fabric (Choose the color depending on your person's skin tone; I usually use tan, pale pink, or white. Batiks are best because they are very finely woven and are easy to draw on.)

Some sample batik colors for various skin colors

Tips

- For this process to succeed and look its best, I highly recommend using batik fabrics. They are very tightly woven and will smoothly absorb all the colors you apply onto them.

- For darker skin tones, don't worry if your fabric is lightly mottled—you will be applying a lot of color to the fabric, and the blotches will disappear.

OUTLINING YOUR BLACK-AND-WHITE PHOTOGRAPH

If your person is fairly large, start by *carefully outlining your person* right on your plain (non-glossy!) black-and-white photo copy using a black medium-point permanent pen. If your person is small with smaller-scale features, use a finer black permanent pen so you don't distort or lose the accuracy of those features.

No matter what size your person is, you will also want to *carefully outline the important details* of their face: eyes, nostrils, ears, lips, eyebrows, neck, and so on. However, *do not outline* the softer details, such as the creases in their cheeks.

It is very important that you try to be as accurate and careful as possible because these outlines will be your guide as you create your person. Pay attention! If the outlines around your person's eyes make them look like blurry blobs, that is exactly how they will look when you try to draw them on the fabric!

If you will be including your person's hands and feet, you will also want to outline their arms, fingers and fingernails, legs, and toes and toenails.

Rosa's black-and-white photograph and her outlined photocopy

2 ## MAKING YOUR PAPER DOLL

Now you are ready to make what I call a Paper Doll. Using a black permanent pen, take a piece of fusible interfacing and trace the *entire outline* of your person onto it, glue side up. (It's easier to draw on the slicker side.) If you accidentally draw on the other side, don't worry: It's not a problem!

You *do not* need to duplicate the facial features on your Paper Doll, but you may want to indicate where the arms, legs, and clothing items (skirt or pants, blouse or shirt, shoes, and the like) are as reference points for when it is time to dress your Paper Doll.

Cut out your Paper Doll and *set it aside*.

The advantage of having this Paper Doll as the foundation on which to "build" your person is that it gives your person stability and will allow you to move your person or people around on your "stage" until you have a composition that looks good to you.

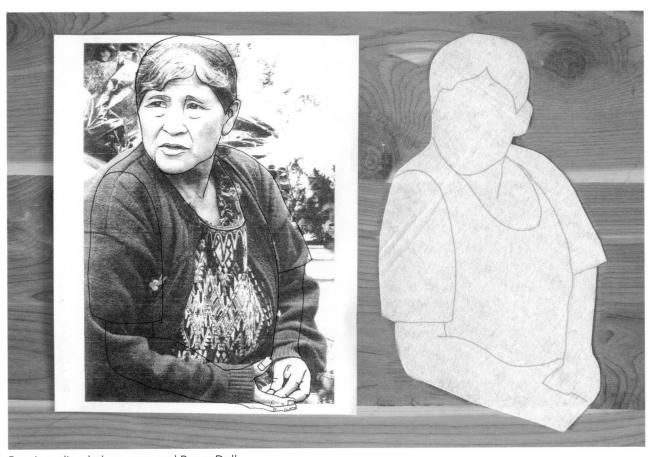

Rosa's outlined photocopy and Paper Doll

A Fusing Your Batik Fabric

Cut a piece of batik fabric that is slightly larger than your person's face and *iron a piece of fusible onto the back*. This will stabilize your batik fabric as you draw on it.

As you draw, you may discover that parts of your fabric have begun to separate and pull away from the fusible backing. If that happens, go back to your ironing board and fuse it down again.

3 DRAWING YOUR PERSON

A Outlining Your Person in Blue Pencil

Start by *working only from your black-and-white photo* so you will not be distracted by skin tones. Place your black-and-white outlined photo on a lightbox or tape it to a bright window; then place or tape your piece of fused batik fabric *side up* over it.

Using a blue colored pencil, carefully transfer all the features that you outlined on your person's face onto the fused fabric, being very sure to *accurately* record them.

If your person has a tan or darker skin tone, like Rosa, use a dark blue pencil. If they are lighter-skinned, use a light blue pencil and a much lighter touch.

NOTE: WHY YOU SHOULD START WITH BLUE PENCIL

What you're about to do is based on a Renaissance technique in which artists made a blue or red-brown underpainting of their subject. The purpose was to create the appearance of a three-dimensional sculpture of facial structure. Once that was completed, they added thin, transparent glazes of color over the underpainting to bring it to life. You will be doing this with colored pencils, and this is where the fun begins. You're about to see your person come alive!

Rosa's blue outline on batik fabric

B Drawing the Shadows

Carefully study your original black-and-white copied photo. Concentrate on the shadows. *Observe and analyze.* Where do the shadows occur on your person's face, neck, and shoulders? Where are they the lightest? Where are they the darkest? Do not take anything for granted!

With the same blue pencil that you used for your outline, draw on your fabric with the side of your pencil or a rounded—not sharp—point. Begin adding shadows in the same places where they occur in your black-and-white photo, such as the shadowed side of the nose, neck, and side of the face.

Proceed with caution. You can always make an area darker later on, but once you have made it too dark, it is much harder to erase the color from your fabric. Contrast the darkest areas—for example, on the neck below the chin—with the lighter areas, like the shadows on the cheeks, which won't require nearly as much shading as the neck.

Take plenty of time to add blue color slowly and carefully. There's no need to rush! If you are working on a Caucasian person, apply color very lightly with a light blue pencil.

Be sure to stop drawing every now and then to check in. Are your shadows in the right places? Are the dark areas dark enough, and are the light areas light enough? If you are not sure, take a photo with your phone.

Continue to *observe and analyze* your black-and-white photograph. When you are finished, stand back. You will suddenly see a three-dimensional "sculpture" of your person's face!

Rosa's face with blue penciled shadows next to her black-and-white photograph

C Adding Color

Now that you are satisfied with the shadows and your person's face looks three-dimensional, let's add color to make your person come alive!

Set aside your black-and-white photograph, and take out your color photo and the rest of your colored pencils.

Observe and analyze:
Disregarding white highlights, what colors are in your person's face that are not in your batik fabric? To test this, choose a colored pencil and hold its point up to your color photograph. Does that color blend in with the photo? If it does, you know that you have chosen well.

Rosa's color photograph, blue face, and colored pencils

If your person has tan or darker skin tones, you will need to add several layers of color: perhaps more brown for the skin, tan or ochre layers, rose red on the cheeks and lips, and maybe even a faint blush around the eyes. If your person is lighter skinned, you will need a whole lot less color and a much lighter touch.

Go slowly, and take time to add color bit by bit and layer by layer. For every color you use, make sure you also *go over every single blue outline* with that color so the blue outlines blend into your person's face and don't stand out. But don't add any color to your person's eyes!

Continue to *observe and analyze* by very carefully studying your color photograph as you continue to draw.

Feel free to color outside the lines, especially on any part of your person's face that will be covered by clothing. You will need a little extra wiggle room in case the clothing doesn't quite line up the way you expected it to, and, unless your person is going to be appliquéd on top of the tulle, you will be cutting right around the outline of your person's face. So it will not matter if the colors you apply end up spreading outside the outlines.

At this stage, there are a few things to keep in mind:

- Be very careful that you don't apply any of these color layers to the eyes!

- Stop every now and then to take a picture of your project or pin up your person's face on your design wall. This will give you a different perspective on your person.

Rosa with single light ochre layer of color

Rosa with brown layer over light ochre layer

D Adding Highlights

When you are satisfied that you have fully developed your person's skin tones, it is time to add highlights to their face.

Observe and analyze: Where do those highlights occur on your color photograph?

Use a white pencil to apply the highlights to your drawing, blending the white into the existing skin tones and making them brighter where necessary: perhaps on the bridge of the nose, the cheeks, the lower lip, and other areas.

Rosa's face with highlights added

E The Final Spark: Making the Eyes Come Alive

It has been said that the eyes are the window into a person's soul. Now that you have brought color to the rest of your person's face, it is time to complete the eyes.

In order to make the eyes come alive, use your white pencil to fill in the white areas on either side of the iris. Then color the iris itself, adding a black circle in the center of the iris and a round white highlight somewhere on the iris to add that final spark of life. You can also use the tip of a toothpick and white paint to create that spark. If your photo does not show a highlight in your person's eyes, add one anyway. You will be glad you did!

Next, depending on your person's complexion, use your black or brown fine permanent marker to draw in the eyelashes. Then draw some hairs on your person's eyebrows.

Look at your person's face. *Observe and analyze!*

- Do you have the right-color skin tones, or do you need to add more color?

- Are the highlights showing up to give even more dimension to the face?

- How about the eyes? Are they filled with light, and do they look alive?

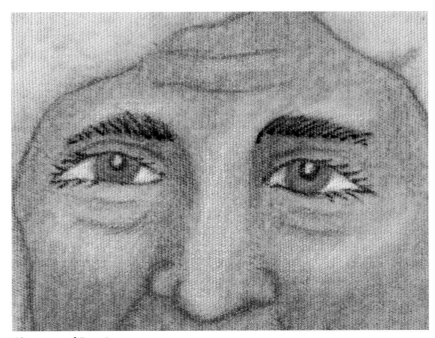

Close-up of Rosa's eyes

4 FIXING YOUR DRAWING

In this step you will be using the spray fixative. It is a wonderful tool, but it is also a health hazard. You must use it in a very well-ventilated place, preferably outside. Be sure to shake up the can thoroughly before you apply spray.

Place your drawing on a sheet of paper or newspaper, and spray on a mist of fixative until your fabric looks slightly damp. Step away and give your drawing a chance to dry thoroughly. Depending on how warm it is outside, this could take an hour or so.

Once your drawing is dry, you can take it back to your work area and check it out. *Observe and analyze.* How does your person look?

There have been times when I realized that my person's face needed more color or highlights. If that happens to you, you can go right back in and draw on the spray-coated fabric! When you are satisfied with your additions, take your drawing back outside and spray on more fixative. Wait for it to dry, and then take another look. If necessary, you can repeat this step as many times as you want.

Rosa's completed face with spray fixative applied

There have been a number of occasions when I was not satisfied with my person's face and had to start drawing him or her all over again. This was especially true of the two people in *Arlington Row in Bibury Village, the Cotswolds, England* (page 26). I must have redrawn each of them at least five times!

So don't be discouraged if you don't get it right on your first try. I promise you that the more people you make, the easier this process will become. It is just a matter of patience and learning how to outline and observe accurately.

Detail of two musicians in *Arlington Row in Bibury Village, the Cotswolds, England* (See full quilt, page 26.)

OTHER BODY PARTS

Now repeat this Paper Doll–making process for the rest of your person's body parts. Be sure to extend the color a bit farther on every body part that is going to be covered by clothing, such as an upper arm that will be placed under a sleeve.

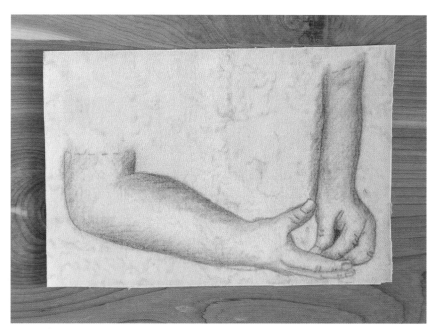

Rosa's blue arms

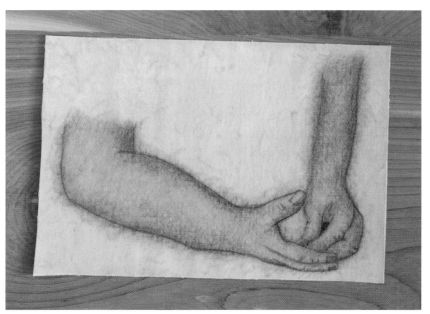

Rosa's arms with extended color

PUTTING YOUR PERSON TOGETHER

Now you can begin putting your person together. Depending on whether the people are beneath the tulle layer or on top of it, there are different steps to take. The reason for placing a figure on top of the tulle is so that he or she will appear to be closer to the viewer than the rest of your landscape; under the tulle, the scene's details appear farther away.

If your person or people are going to be placed *under* your final tulle layer, you can cut right up to the edges of your person's body parts and clothing as you go. But if you are going to appliqué your person on *top* of the tulle, you will need to leave at least a ¼˝ margin all around the edges of your person. In this way, you will be able to turn under the edges of your person when you appliqué them down.

In *Flower Market at Chichicastenango, Guatemala* (page 64), I placed Rosa on top of the tulle. Therefore, when I made this quilt, I left an extra margin of fabric all around her, including her hair. She was appliquéd down. If you look at the women behind her, who are all behind the black tulle, I have cut right up to the edge of each of their Paper Dolls, including their clothing and hair.

If your person is going to be placed on top of the tulle, you can do all the machine stitching right on your Paper Doll *before* you appliqué it down. If your person will be placed *under* the tulle, you do not need to do any machine stitching at this time.

Detail of several Guatemalan women in *Flower Market at Chichicastenango, Guatemala* (See full quilt, page 64.)

A The Face

Begin dressing your Paper Doll, starting with your person's face.

In this exercise, unlike in the *Flower Market* quilt, I have prepared Rosa to be placed *under* the final tulle layer.

I. Cut right around the edge of your drawing, including the hair. *Be sure to leave at least an extra ¼″ margin around any part of your person that's going to be covered by clothing!*

2. Peel off the fusible paper backing and apply your person's face directly onto her Paper Doll.

If your fusible glue is a bit sticky, such as with Lite Steam-A-Seam 2, you do not need to iron the face down yet. But if the face will not stay put, you can touch it lightly with your iron to secure it in place.

3. Check your placement. Turn your Paper Doll over and see if your drawing is bigger than your Paper Doll. If it is slightly larger, don't worry. You can either leave it as is or trim it down to match the back side of the Paper Doll.

Note that I have left extra fabric below Rosa's neck. I want to have a bit of wiggle room when I place her blouse on my Paper Doll.

Rosa's face cut out and placed on her Paper Doll

B The Arms

Place your person's arms on your Paper Doll, but be sure *not* to iron them down. You will need to slip them over and under her clothing!

The upper part of Rosa's arms will need to be positioned *under her blouse sleeves*, but the lower part of her arms will be *on top of* her blouse, which is why I have not ironed them down.

Placing but not fusing down Rosa's arms on the Paper Doll

C Dressing the Paper Doll

It's time to dress your Paper Doll!

I. Using my full-size black-and-white photograph, I made freezer-paper templates of both sleeves and also the front of Rosa's blouse and her hair.

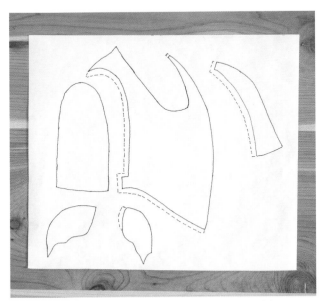

Freezer-paper templates of Rosa's clothing and hair

 Tip I always draw a dotted line on my pattern pieces to remind myself where to add extra fabric to the parts that will extend under the adjacent clothing or body part.

2. The cut-out freezer-paper pattern pieces can now be positioned on the fabric you have chosen for your person's clothing. When you know where you want your pattern pieces to be on the clothing fabric, iron them down, cut out those chunks of fabric, and iron fusible onto the back of them. Now you can carefully cut out the blouse front and both sleeves.

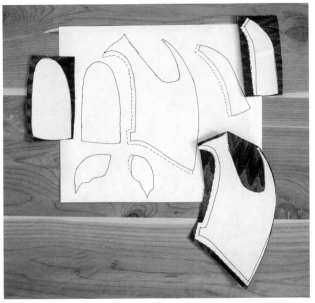

Freezer-paper templates, before and after being applied to fabric

Notice how I have left a ¼˝ margin on the left side of Rosa's sleeve where it will be *tucked under* the right side of her blouse front. I have also left a ¼˝ margin on the left side of the blouse front, where it will be *overlapped* by the left arm and sleeve.

3. Next, I have applied the parts of Rosa's blouse to her Paper Doll, making sure to place the tops of her arms *under* the sleeves, and the lower part of her arms *over* her blouse front. Do the same for your own person.

If you turn your Paper Doll over and discover that some of the clothing sticks out over the edges of the Paper Doll, you can trim it down to size if desired, but it may look fine just the way it is.

D Hair

The kind of hair you choose for your person's head can vary. If your person is going to be under tulle, you can use anything you like: more fabric, roving, or yarn. In Rosa's case, I have used black satin fabric.

In the same way that you have made your person's clothing, you will also make a freezer-paper template for your person's hair.

In Rosa's case, I applied a fusible to the back of the hair fabric because satin tends to shred. I could have taken advantage of this, however, by allowing the shreds to represent wisps of hair around Rosa's face.

There are a few things to think about when dealing with hair:

- If you are making hair (or clothing) that has folds or pleats in it, cut a larger piece of fabric and iron folds into it. Iron fusible to the back of it to set the folds. Now you can iron your freezer-paper template piece onto the folded and fused hair (or clothing) fabric and cut out the entire hair shape. Remove the fusible backing and place the hair in the appropriate location on your Paper Doll's head.

- If your person has long hair or yarn hair, you may need to tuck parts of it behind their shoulders or drape it across their neck and chest.

You can now iron down and fuse every part of your person onto your Paper Doll.

Completed Rosa with clothing and hair

7 CREATING A WHOLE PERSON

A whole person is created exactly the same way, but you will have to make more body parts: legs, feet, and clothing. All of the whole people in my quilts are put together in this same way. It's fun to make skirts, pants, and shoes!

Las Mujeres Azules de Guatemala (The Blue Ladies of Guatemala) (page 82) demonstrates another excellent reason to make Paper Dolls of your people, and this is where I first developed my Paper Doll Technique. Although this quilt does not have a tulle overlay, it does use tulle to create the shadows beneath the women's feet, which anchor them to the ground.

I began the quilt by creating the stage for the women to stand on. I then constructed and dressed each of them individually, draping their lovely fabrics and hand-crafted belts all around them. As each woman was completed, I placed her on my stage, moving her around in relation to every new arrival until I was satisfied with the way the whole group interacted with each other and with the viewer. Once I had arrived at a satisfactory composition, I hand-appliquéd all of the women in place and stitched their clothing onto the quilt, allowing many parts of the fabric to hang free as a three-dimensional visual element.

Original photo of one Blue Lady in *Las Mujeres Azules de Guatemala (The Blue Ladies of Guatemala)* (page 82)   *Photo by Meri Henriques Vahl*

Dressing first Paper Doll in *Las Mujeres Azules de Guatemala (The Blue Ladies of Guatemala)* (See full quilt, page 82.)   *Photo by Meri Henriques Vahl*

Two dressed Paper Dolls in *Las Mujeres Azules de Guatemala (The Blue Ladies of Guatemala)* (See full quilt, page 82.)   *Photo by Meri Henriques Vahl*

Two dressed Paper Dolls joining their undressed Paper Doll friends in *Las Mujeres Azules de Guatemala (The Blue Ladies of Guatemala)* (See full quilt, page 82.)   *Photo by Meri Henriques Vahl*

Las Mujeres Azules de Guatemala (The Blue Ladies of Guatemala), 60″ × 48″, by Meri Henriques Vahl

Notice that I've chosen to reorganize how the ladies are finally grouped on their stage.

For an article of clothing that has folds in it, such as a skirt, put fusible on a larger piece of fabric, peel off the paper backing, and work with the fabric, adding the folds where appropriate. Don't worry about trying to fit your fabric exactly to the shape of your skirt. Simply place it on your Paper Doll in the appropriate location, and then iron it down. Make sure you put a piece of resist paper underneath

the Paper Doll to keep the excess fused fabric from sticking to your ironing board!

Once the pleated fabric is fused onto your Paper Doll, you can turn your Paper Doll over and trim the article of clothing down to size using the back of your Paper Doll as a guide. Sometimes I like the way the clothing looks without trimming and I'll leave it as is.

Take a look at the whole people in *Dawn Prayers on the Ganges* (page 90) and *Free Tibet* (page 36).

Detail of people in traditional dress in *Free Tibet* (See full quilt, page 36.)

Once you have carefully ironed your entire person to secure all of their parts in place, you are ready to put that person or people anywhere you want in your completed landscape. Don't forget to position some navy-blue tulle beneath your person's feet so they don't look like they are floating off the ground!

When you are satisfied with the placement of your Paper Doll, you can add a bit of glue or a narrow strip of fusible to the back of it, especially to the legs. This will hold both the person and its tulle shadow in place until you are ready to stitch.

Not only can you use this method to create people but you can also make a Paper Doll for anything else that you wish to put in your quilt. In *Free Tibet* (page 36), I made Paper Dolls for all of the people, both palaces, and even the yak, which I covered in strips of yarn that were secured in place when I did the stitching over the final layer of black tulle.

8 ## THE PAPER DOLL TECHNIQUE EXPANDED

You will no doubt find that the Paper Doll Technique you just used for making people is a wonderful tool for other elements of your quilt. The technique came in handy for me especially while making *The Basket Makers of Axoum, Ethiopia.*

When a travel brochure unexpectedly arrived in my mailbox, I was immediately captivated by the image of a lovely young woman carrying a beautiful woven basket that was almost as big as she was. The basket displayed similar vibrant colors that had attracted me to Guatemalan fabric. An internet search revealed an area in northern Ethiopia that is famous for its craftspeople who weave baskets of all sizes and shapes; the local folk use the baskets in their homes and also market to tourists. Naturally, I had to make a quilt!

Dragging out my stash of striped Guatemalan fabric, I proceeded to cut it into strips and then into lots of little triangles, which I fused onto basket-shaped Paper Dolls. I placed the resulting baskets in the marketplace landscape I had already assembled on my worktable. People soon followed, including some whose hair I made with strands of black crinkled yarn. The quilt was definitely taking shape, and, before long, Paper Doll chickens began arriving! As is my custom, I completed the quilt with a border of culturally themed fabric. In this case, that involved lots of vivid African prints set off by beading and a zebra-striped binding.

Detail of chicken and baskets in *The Basket Makers of Axoum, Ethiopia* (See full quilt, at right.)

Detail of yarn applied as hair in *The Basket Makers of Axoum, Ethiopia* (See full quilt, below.)

The Basket Makers of Axoum, Ethiopia, 74″ × 51″, by Meri Henriques Vahl

9 A WORD ABOUT ARCHITECTURE

The human eye is every bit as fussy about wanting architecture to look believable as it is about the human figure. I have found that the Paper Doll Technique is the best way to achieve perfect-looking architecture for my quilts. Using full-size black-and-white photographs, I can make freezer-paper templates of the required building elements, both exterior and interior, and also create as many Paper Dolls as are needed to make realistic-looking buildings, no matter how complicated they may appear to be.

We All Speak Peace, 48½″ × 58″, by Meri Henriques Vahl

When I discovered a photograph of a lovely Blue Mosque in a magazine article, I was inspired by the mood and sentiment of the place. I immediately knew that I wanted to make a quilt of it. The architecture was gorgeous and challenging, and the interplay of light and shadow was very interesting. I did not want to steal someone else's work, however, so I altered some of the interior details and pared down the crowd of people who were there that day to just three, subtly changing the way they looked.

A trip to my local photocopying store and the use of their biggest printer provided me with a large black-and-white copy on plain paper that was just the size I wanted. From that I was able to make freezer-paper templates and Paper Dolls of the three women and some of the trickier parts of the roof structure.

Various batik fabrics were perfect for the ceiling design patterns, which eventually required a great deal of stitching to do them justice (especially after my daughter's cat decided to climb up the quilt, tearing holes as he went, which I eventually had to spend many hours repairing!).

When the central scene was done, the finishing touch was to create a hand-quilted batik border decorated with the hand-appliquéd words *Shalom Aleichem* (Hebrew), *Assalamu Aleikum* (Arabic), *Om Mani Padme Hum* (Tibetan), and *Peace Be Unto You*—all of which express the same sentiment. And I believe that no matter what the language in which those words are spoken, people all over the world truly desire peace.

Detail of Blue Mosque ceiling in *We All Speak Peace* (See full quilt, previous page.)

A Window and Building Treatments

The best way to make windows is to cut out the shape of the entire window from one piece of fabric. For example, cut a large piece of white to include the whole window plus the outside trim, and then add on smaller squares to represent the window panes. The result of doing this is that you will not have to wrestle with tiny, hard-to-make window trim pieces!

This is what I did for the buildings in *Dawn Prayers on the Ganges* (page 90), *Free Tibet* (page 36), and *Arlington Row in Bibury Village, the Cotswolds, England* (page 26), and it is also a good approach to consider when you are making any kind of structure.

For example, if your landscape contains a house, make a freezer-paper template that includes all of the details—doors, windows, roof, and the like—so you can use them later when you are ready to construct the necessary elements of the structure. Next, make a Paper Doll of the building's *entire shape*, including the roof, chimney, and any gables. Now you are ready to dress your building.

Decide which color appears on most of your house. Let's say it is white. Iron fusible onto the back of a white fabric piece, and iron that piece directly onto the front of your *entire building*, making sure you don't accidentally fuse it onto your ironing board or iron.

Turn the Paper Doll over and, using it as a guide, cut out the shape of the house. You now have a ghostly all-white building! Next, choose a roof material, iron your freezer-paper roof template onto it, and apply fusible on the back. Cut out the roof and fuse it onto the house.

Tip Shadow Treatment

Here's a trick to use if there are shadowed parts of your house that extend all the way up a wall to the roof. Instead of adding on another darker piece of fabric to represent a shadowed wall, you can cut some navy blue tulle to cover the shadowed area or areas. Do this before you fuse down the roof fabric. Make sure the tulle is long enough to extend all the way up under where you intend to place the roof. Set the tulle shadow in the appropriate location and carefully iron down the roof to secure the shadow in place.

Construct the windows, doors, and any other parts of your building as described above.

Your goal should always be to try to come up with the simplest, most direct way to tackle any design issues that you will inevitably encounter along the way. Unlike traditional pieced quilting, you don't have to laboriously fit together the many individual parts of a building, tree, or structure. Just figure out the best, most straightforward way to create the items you need for your quilt.

Detail of Tibetan Palace in *Free Tibet* (See full quilt, page 36.)

OVERVIEW OF THE PAPER DOLL TECHNIQUE

Now that you know the basic techniques of building a quilt scene, including landscapes, people, and architecture, let's go through the construction of a quilt from start to finish to see how comprehensive

Dawn Prayers on the Ganges, 46½″ × 80″, by Meri Henriques Vahl

the Paper Doll Technique can be. This is especially evident in *Dawn Prayers on the Ganges*, a very complex scene that won me my second Best Quilts of the World award in 2011.

In the case of this quilt, I was inspired by the many photographs I had seen of the gorgeous colors and beautiful people of India. I wanted to create a vista that would represent the ambiance and lively activity that occurs when pilgrims from all over their country travel to their sacred Mother Ganges River to pray, bathe, and make offerings to their gods. The challenge was finding the right photographs that I could combine together to represent my impression of a particular location through its architecture and people.

Once I was sure of the landscape and before I started constructing any of the river scene, I cut wedges from a wonderful striped batik fabric and laid them out in a fan shape across the whole sky area. I began the landscape itself with the distant left-hand riverbank, cutting out and placing several buildings before applying a layer of rosy pink tulle over them to push them back into the distance.

Detail of batik sky and distant river buildings in *Dawn Prayers on the Ganges* (See full quilt, page 90.)

Working forward from there and adding more pink tulle as I went along, I made individual templates, my Paper Dolls, for each structure along the riverbank until I reached the steps. Now it was time to make Paper Dolls of the buildings above the steps, creating their shadows and three-dimensionality with Caran d'Ache watercolor pencils and strips of navy blue tulle. Before I added the actual steps, I fanned out more of that lovely striped batik fabric in the foreground and laid a layer of watery, rippled rainbow lamé over them.

Detail of buildings above steps in *Dawn Prayers on the Ganges* (See full quilt, page 90.)

Once the steps were installed, I had fun finding people from many different photographs and deciding how and where to arrange them on the steps. The foreground women were the most rewarding of all. As I created and completed each foreground Paper Doll, I made her body extra long, slit the lamé river fabric, and inserted her partway into the water to create her underwater reflection. Having completed this step, it was time to add the final layer of black tulle and quilt the project.

Detail of woman in water and steps in *Dawn Prayers on the Ganges* (See full quilt, page 90.)

After I had steamed and squared up my quilt, I added borders of dupioni silk and antique brocade sari trims. Only then was it possible to undertake the beading on their clothing and the Mylar water streaming down from their hands, sparkling with beaded accents.

Detail of Dupioni silk border in *Dawn Prayers on the Ganges* (See full quilt, page 90.)

Detail of women in water in *Dawn Prayers on the Ganges* (See full quilt, page 90.)

Finishing Your Quilt: Borders, Binding, and More!

Now that you have finished stitching and squaring up your fabric collage (with or without people in it), you are ready to add borders or even more quilt! First, we will discuss adding a simple border. You may be asking yourself how this is accomplished when the quilt is trimmed and doesn't have additional backing. The answer is that borders are attached to *both* the front and back simultaneously and batting is fused in between. You might say you are duplicating the border on the back of your project. Let's get started to see how this works!

MATERIALS

- Batting
- Fabric for front borders
- Fabric for back borders
- Ruler, rotary cutter, and cutting mat
- Straight pins
- Fusible webbing: ½˝-wide roll (Stitch Witchery by Dritz, for example)

Note: Please read through all instructions first before proceeding.

CUTTING THE BORDERS

1. Start by measuring the 2 *longest sides* of your quilt. This can be either the width or the length, depending on the orientation of your project. Add at least 2˝ to that measurement to give yourself a little wiggle room.

2. Decide how wide you want your borders to be, taking into account that you'll be adding a binding once your borders are applied. Add an extra ¼˝ to that width measurement for attaching your border strips to the quilt body. For example, if you decide on a 3˝-wide border, the formula looks like this: 3˝ + ¼˝ (binding) + ¼˝ (seam allowance) = 3½˝-wide cut border strips.

3. Select fabric for your front and back borders. They don't have to be the same. Using the measurements you have decided upon, cut the following pieces:

- 2 long border strips from front border fabric
- 2 long border strips from back border fabric
- 2 pieces of long border batting *that are just as long but ½˝ narrower* than the cut width of your borders

Squared-up quilt with front and back long border strips and batting, and short front and back border strips and batting. I provided separate border strips and batting strips for this photograph.

CONSTRUCTING THE FIRST BORDER

1. Start on the back of your quilt. Place a long back-border strip in place *facedown* along one long edge. Make sure the edge of the border strip aligns with the edge of your quilt. Allow the extra border fabric to extend off both ends of your quilt. Pin the back border in place.

2. Apply the front border in the same manner, making sure that the *right side* of the front-border strip is *facedown* on your quilt. Again, the *long edges* of the borders are even with the *long edge* of your quilt.

3. Stitch a seam ¼˝ away from the long edge of your quilt all the way to the end of the long edge of your quilt.

Front and back long border strips stitched in place with a ¼˝ seam and ironed out

4. Press both border strips away from the main body of the quilt. Then, once again, fold back the top border strip to expose the *wrong side of the back border strip*. Cut a strip of ¼″ fusible webbing (such as Stitch Witchery by Dritz) the approximate length of the quilt's long edge. Lay it down on the wrong side of the back border strip, right next to the previously squared-up long edge of the quilt.

5. Lay a strip of batting on the back border strip on top of the fusible webbing. Butt it *right up against*, but not on, the squared-up long edge of the quilt.

Long front border strip folded back and batting strip placed on top of long back border strip

6. Place another strip of fusible webbing on top of the batting. Position the top border strip over the batting and webbing. Iron the long border thoroughly to melt the fusible and secure all strips and batting firmly in place.

7. Repeat Steps 1–6 on the opposite long border, using the remaining long back- and front-border strips and the remaining batting strip to construct the other long border in exactly the same way.

8. Place the quilt on your cutting mat to trim the excess long border fabric. Lay the ruler along the *short* edge of the quilt and over both long borders. Once again, square up the quilt with the rotary cutter.

All long borders stitched on, and batting added and squared up

 Tip Be sure to add the long borders first. If you apply the shorter borders first, the long borders will have become even longer and harder to control when you are ready to add them!

ADDING THE SHORT BORDERS

1. Measure the short sides of your quilt. They will be longer because they also include the width of the 2 borders you have already added. Add a couple of extra inches to the length.

2. Cut 4 border strips and 2 batting strips according to Cutting the Borders, Steps 1–3 (page 96).

3. Repeat Constructing the First Border, Steps 1–8 (pages 97 and 98).

ANOTHER BORDER TECHNIQUE

I often make fancy pieced front borders for my quilts, and I am not always sure how they are going to mesh with the dimensions of the squared-up quilt. To make sure everything comes out looking good, I attach *only the 4 back-border strips and all the batting to the backside* of my landscape. I follow the same process described in Constructing the First Border, Steps 1–5 (pages 97 and 98). After fusing the batting to the borders, I turn my quilt *right side* up and add fusible webbing on top of the exposed batting.

All four borders squared up and quilt ready for binding

Next, I lay the pieced borders right on top of the batting and fusible webbing. I butt them up against the ¼″ line of stitching on the front of my quilt and make any necessary adjustments. Once I am satisfied with my placement, I fuse all of the pieced front borders in place. *But at this point, I do not stitch them down.*

Next, I apply a narrow ribbon or other trim piece with a very narrow ¼″ fusible webbing strip underneath it to secure it in place. This will effectively cover and disguise the ¼″ stitch line and the ¼″ seam allowance of the pieced border. Once I have ironed this cover trim in place, I stitch it down. I can now complete any necessary quilting on the border itself. To finish, I add my binding, all of the beaded embellishments, and a 4″ sleeve for hanging up the finished quilt.

Border detail in *Flower Market at Chichicastenango, Guatemala* (See full quilt, page 64.)

SOME ADDITIONAL THOUGHTS

An exciting thing about the technique you have just learned is that it's extremely flexible. Instead of immediately adding borders and finishing your quilt, you can use this same method to enlarge your quilt by stitching on larger pieces of quilt-back fabric and batting. Once your original quilt is stitched, steamed, and squared up, and before you create the borders, you can add *a whole new section of any size* onto your original landscape and completely change the way it looks!

For example, before you add any borders, you could turn your original *Grand Tetons Revisited* quilt (page 45) into a view out of a cabin window by adding a wall or even a whole room around it. You would only have to stitch on the newly added portions, since the original landscape is already finished! Once your new section was collaged, covered in tulle, and stitched, you could go ahead and add borders and binding as described on the previous pages.

When I first learned the basics of this technique from Northern California quilter Laura Fogg, she showed us a fairly small horizontal landscape she had made that depicted the sky, some distant ocean, and a foreground meadow. After she had stitched and squared it up, she decided it didn't hold enough interest, so she added a very large piece of quilt back and batting to the lower edge of her original quilt. She then proceeded to embellish this new section with a foreground deck and railing, a couple of Adirondack chairs, and several pots of colorful flowers—all of it looking out over what was now a very peaceful view! With the addition of tulle, a second round of quilting on the new section, and four borders, she now had an interesting and truly lovely quilt.

FINISHING TOUCHES

You are now ready to add binding. Once you have done so, your quilt is nearly finished!

1. Follow your preferred binding method for your quilt.

2. Add any hard embellishments, such as beads, to your quilt.

3. Cut and sew on a 4˝ sleeve.

4. Hang up your finished quilt and admire it!

A Gallery of Student Quilts: You Can Do It, Too!

Here are some of the wonderful quilts that my many talented students have made. It was the first time any of them had worked with the Fabric Collage with Tulle Overlay and Paper Doll techniques, and I am so proud of them!

Still Life: Vase of Flowers, 36″ × 50″, by Diana McClun

Venice Becomes Manarola, 44″ × 47″, by Nikki Vilas

The new moon, peering through the pine trees,

saw plovers scudding along a sandy shore.

A haiku by Ho-o

Plovers in the Moonlight: An Illustrated Haiku, 42″ × 19½″, by Barbara Beer

Waiting at Agora, 26″ × 27″, by Ann Waskey

Melk, Austria, 26″ × 36″, by Phyliss A. Lewis

Garden Walk, Mom and Dad, 21½″ × 29″, by Phyliss A. Lewis

Chicas de Fuego (Girls of Fuego), 25″ × 29″, by Cyndy Lyle Rymer

The Notice, 23¾″ × 15½″, by Lynne Nostrant

Daddy and Jackson, 11″ × 14″, by Lynne Nostrant

Daddy and Reese, 11″ × 14″, by Lynne Nostrant

About the Author

MERI HENRIQUES VAHL lives in the Santa Cruz, California, area with her family and two rowdy felines. Descended from many generations of artists, she graduated from the University of California, Berkeley with a degree in fine art, which she quickly realized would not put a paycheck in her hand or food in her stomach. Although both of her parents, who were school teachers, encouraged her to get a teaching credential based on the theory that teachers can always find a job, Meri swore that she would never teach anyone anything.

Photo by Jim Vahl

Furthermore, she had previously made another personal vow when, upon entering the seventh grade, she discovered that girls were not allowed to take woodshop as their elective. Instead, she was shunted into a home economics class, where she learned how to make English muffin pizzas and apply makeup. She was eventually given the choice of using a sewing machine to make either an apron (no way!) or a sailor blouse. Thoroughly disgusted with the whole fiasco, Meri made the following vow: "I'm never going to wear makeup or use a sewing machine ever again!" It wasn't until years later that she discovered that her name is Hebrew for "rebellious." She will leave it up to her friends and students to decide just how successful a rebel she has been!

In the mid-1990s, after discovering the exciting world of art quilting and developing her own unique method of creating people to inhabit her quilts, Meri was encouraged by her friend Ellen Edith to begin a rewarding career of teaching others how to use her favorite techniques in their own art quilts. Meri taught under the auspices of Diana McClun, founder of Empty Spools Seminars at Asilomar, California. She has since had the good fortune to lecture and teach at quilt guilds all over northern and central California; at Pacific International Quilt Festival in Santa Clara, California; in Nevada, France, and Australia; and of course, at Empty Spools Seminars.

Always inspired by her awesome students and the amazing work of her fellow art quilters, Meri has made a number of award-winning quilts, including three that won the Mancuso Brothers' Best Quilts of the World Fest in 2009, 2011, and 2015. She encourages her students—whether advanced or beginner—to enjoy the process of making art, to allow themselves to let go of their preconceived notions of how quilts "have to be made," and to play with the fabric.

You can see more of Meri's work on her website. Her memoir, *Hoosier Hysteria: A Fateful Year in the Crosshairs of Race in America*, about her freshman year of college at Indiana University in 1963, is available in local bookstores and on Amazon.

Visit Meri online and follow on social media!

WEBSITE: meriartquilts.com • **FACEBOOK:** /merihenriquesvahlauthor